Poetry Bridges

Poetry Bridges
うたの架け橋

Canberra/Nara Commemorative Anthology
キャンベラ・奈良記念作品集

**Edited by Saeko Ogi
Amelia Fielden
and Noriko Tanaka**

Poetry Bridges: Canberra/Nara Commemorative Anthology
ISBN 978 1 76041 628 7
Copyright © this collection Saeko Ogi and Amelia Fielden 2018
Copyright © poems individual contributors 2018
Cover designed by Saeko Ogi and Mari Uchida

First published 2018 by
GINNINDERRA PRESS
PO Box 3461 Port Adelaide 5015
www.ginninderrapress.com.au

キャンベラ篇

Canberra Compilation

edited by Amelia Fielden
with Japanese translations by Saeko Ogi

Anne Benjamin

under the dome
of the War Memorial
the chatter
of schoolchildren
folds into a hush

アン・ベンジャミン

戦争記念館の
ドームをくぐる
児童らの
交わすおしゃべり
沈黙となる

Michelle Brock

new exhibition
at the National Gallery
Madonna and Child
on dew-covered grass
a kangaroo feeds her joey

ミシェル・ブロック

美術館に
聖母子画の
飾らるる
露ふふむ草に
乳やるカンガルー

Owen Bullock

eucalypt leaves
blue in red dust

オーエン・ブーロック

紅の塵に
ユーカリの葉の青

Robyn Christmas   ロビン・クリスマス

memory –   東大寺へ
squeezing through Buddha's nostril   行きし日思う
in the Tōdaiji   大仏の
enlightenment comes   鼻腔抜ければ
but when...   悟るとぞ いつ

PS Cottier   PS コティエ

bicycle paths   閑静な
connecting quiet suburbs   地区を結べる
gentle progress   自転車道
she parts a white sea   鸚鵡の白き
flock of cockatoos   海を分けゆく

Barbara Curnow   バーバラ・カーナウ

wooden crates   友よりて
of apples and pears   林檎を梨を
shared with friends –   分け合いぬ
Fyshwick Markets   六十年代
nineteen sixties   フィシュウィック市場

Lee Davy   リー・デイヴィ

our bush capital   ブッシュ・キャピタル
kangaroos roam around   カンガルー彷徨い
wild parrots abound   鸚鵡のあまた

Jan Dobb

a mother
pushes a pram of twins –
Canberra/Nara Park

ジャン・ドブ

母親と
乳母車の双子
キャンベラ奈良公園

Tess Driver

surrounded
with parks and bird song
a special place
built to a design
and a planner's dream

テス・ドライヴァ

鳥の声
聞く公園の
数多なる
設計家の
夢成就の地

Amelia Fielden

(Nara Park)

a solo stag
lame in one hind leg
slowly follows
its herd disappearing
into the dusky hills

アメリア・フィールデン

「奈良公園にて」

後足を
牡鹿引きずり
ゆっくりと
群れに従きつつ
夕丘に消ゆ

Beverley George　　　　　　　　ベヴァリー・ジョージ

before the temple　　　　　　　大仏の
in which Great Buddha dwells　　お堂の前に
a woman kneels　　　　　　　　膝をつき
faceless beneath a wide cloth hat　帽の目深き
garden trowel in hand　　　　　　女シャベル手に

David Gilbey　　　　　　　　　デヴィド・ギルビー

lasagne in Japan:　　　　　　　日本のラザニア
don't forget shiitake and soy,　　椎茸に醤油忘るな
fold like a futon　　　　　　　　ふとんに重ね

Jill Gower　　　　　　　　　　ジル・ゴーワー

War Memorial　　　　　　　　朱の芥子の
scarlet poppies ablaze on walls　壁に飾らる
for those fallen　　　　　　　　戦争記念館
in blood-soaked conflicts –　　血の戦場を
Lest We Forget　　　　　　　　我ら忘るな

Margaret Grace

Mount Stromlo
observatory
takes my soul
out into the universe,
shows me my future journey

マーガレット・グレース

ストロムロの
天文台は
魂を
宇宙へ送り
未来の道指す

Janne Graham

pink glow
across the Brindabella
sunset
late cockatoos screech home,
mosquitoes begin to bite

ジャンヌ・グラハム

ブリンダベラを
夕茜染め
騒がしき
鸚鵡は家路へ
蚊の刺し始む

flocks of currawong
move into town in winter –
capital playground

街中へ
クロフエガラス
首都の冬

Hazel Hall　　　　　　　　　　　ヘイズル・ホール

a formal bow　　　　　　　　　　お辞儀して
followed by a handshake　　　　　握手を交わし
and laughter　　　　　　　　　　笑い合う
cherishing friendship　　　　　　　文化二つの
between two cultures　　　　　　　友情つなぐ

Simon Hanson　　　　　　　　　　サイモン・ハンソン

summer breeze　　　　　　　　　夏風や
swirls and waves　　　　　　　　　渦に波立つ
in a sea of bluebells　　　　　　　ブルーベルの海
　　　　　　　　　　　　　　　　（註：ブルーベルはキャンベラ市の花）

golden wattle　　　　　　　　　　黄金のワトルの花や
the red of gang gangs　　　　　　ギャンギャン鸚鵡の紅
on blue sky　　　　　　　　　　　そして青空
　　　　　　　　　　　　　　　　（註：ワトルはアカシア科の花で国花）

Jeffrey Harping　　　　　　　　　ジェフリー・ハーピング

(Canberra/Nara Park)　　　　　　「キャンベラ・奈良公園にて」

by the PEACE　　　　　　　　　　刻まれし
chiseled in stone, a child　　　　　「平和」の文字に
blowing bubbles　　　　　　　　　子のシャボン玉

Lois Holland

morning frost
achingly cold
melts away
into glorious sunshine –
our winter bonus

ロイス・ホランド

冷えまさる
朝霜の
燦燦の日に
溶けゆくさまは
冬のボーナス

Marilyn Humbert

(at Canberra's Botanic Gardens)

in the vaults
of the herbarium
plant specimens
ensure biodiversity
for future generations

マリリン・ハムバート

「キャンベラ植物園にて」

地下室に
並ぶ植物
標本の
生物の未来の
多様を約す

Samantha Sirimanne Hyde

we tiptoe
around the vivid blooms –
after Floriade
their magical touch
extends to the hospice

サマンサ・シリマンヌ・ハイド

鮮やかな花の
めぐりを忍び足
花まつり
魔法の気配
ホスピスに達す
註：'Floriade'はキャンベラの花まつりの名）

Kazuharu Ienaga　　　　　　　　　家永和治

both Canberra and Nara　　　　　キャンベラも奈良も
no smell of tide　　　　　　　　　潮の香のなく
far from sea　　　　　　　　　　　海の隔たる

Gerry Jacobson　　　　　　　　　ジェリー・ジャコブソン

southerly　　　　　　　　　　　　雪払う
wind off the snow　　　　　　　　南風に銅像の
R.G. Menzies　　　　　　　　　　メンジス首相
walks the lunchtime track　　　　　上着ボタンをはめ
buttoned up in his bronze suit　　　昼休みを歩く
　　　　　　　　　　　　　　　　（註：南半球の南風は冷たい）

Julianne Jameson　　　　　　　　ジュリアンヌ・ジェムソン

rising　　　　　　　　　　　　　丘の上に
above the House　　　　　　　　立つ議事堂に
on the hill　　　　　　　　　　　いくつもの
massed hot-air balloons　　　　　朝の軽気球
escape a chilly morning　　　　　寒気を逃る

Ramah Juta　　　　　　　　　　　ラマ・ジュタ

(Nara)　　　　　　　　　　　　　「奈良」

shrine lanterns　　　　　　　　　藤の滝
cascading wisteria　　　　　　　　社の灯りの
radiate peace　　　　　　　　　　平和を照らす

Richard Kakoi　　　　　　　リチャード・カコイ

(January 2003 Canberra bushfires)「2003年キャンベラ山火事」

burning pine trees　　　　　　ストロムロの
around Mount Stromlo　　　　山の松焼く
after the firestorm　　　　　　火の嵐
one telescope survives　　　　星座図を引く
mapping the starry night sky　テレスコープ一本残る

Keitha Keyes　　　　　　　　キーサ・キーズ

this city　　　　　　　　　　この街に
of roundabouts　　　　　　　来れば戸惑う
condemns me　　　　　　　　ロータリー
to confusion　　　　　　　　混乱するは
in traffic and politics　　　　政治に及ぶ

as cherry blossoms　　　　　花の色に
frame this ancient city　　　染まるる古都に
my thoughts turn　　　　　　しのび入る
to family so far away　　　　渦まく紅葉に
in swirling autumn leaves　　遥かな家族

Kate King

magpie neighbours
line their nest,
our dog's hair
a soft cushion
for their dappled eggs

koala joey
swings for the crowd
at Tidbinbilla
a toddler wobbles over
to admiring parents

鵲の
隣人巣をかけ
斑卵の
褥にまじる
我の犬の毛

ティンディンビラの
ちょこちょこ動く
コアラの仔
見惚れる親に
ふらつく子ども

Kathy Kituai　　　　　　　　　　キャシー・キチュエイ

(Canberra/Nara Park Candle Festival)　「キャンベラ・奈良公園 キャンドル祭」

candles
in a dry creek
one wick lit
after the other
all the same, yet...

涸れ川に
蝋燭の火を
灯しゆく
なべては同じ
とはいうものの

origami lesson
in an Aussie tent
folding
two cities
together

折り紙を
豪州テントに
折りており
二つの街の
寄り添いながら

Lorraine Lee-Pearson　　　　　　ロレイン　リー・ピアソン

though oceans apart
always dramatic
entertainment:
Australian politics
and Japanese Kabuki

海原に
隔てられても
楽しかる
ドラマティックな
豪州政治と日本の歌舞伎

Catherine McGrath　　　　　　キャサリン・マグラー

groomed hedges　　　　　　　小綺麗な生垣
abut straight rows of gums　　ユーカリの並木
street after street　　　　　　また並木
this unsettling beauty　　　　飼いならさるる
of nature tamed　　　　　　　自然の不自然美

Margaret Mahony　　　　　　マーガレット・マホニー

wattle burst –　　　　　　　ワトルはじけ
the kookaburra　　　　　　　ワライカワセミ
sets up territory　　　　　　縄張りを張る

Saeko Ogi　　　　　　　　　小城小枝子

clatter, clunk, clunk　　　　　カランコロン
geta sandals hit the floor –　　板前さんは
the Japanese chef　　　　　　下駄脱がず
never takes them off　　　　　床打ち鳴らす
in his Canberra restaurant　　キャンベラの店

Greg Piko

in my heart
I'm a squawking galah
hanging from a wire
wings spread to catch the rain
on my fluffy pink belly

グレッグ・ピーコ

胸内の
我姦ましきギャラーなり
電線宙づり翼を広げ
ふわふわお腹に
雨受け止める
(註：galah は鸚鵡の一種)

Sandra Renew

driving to Cooma
across the Monaro plains
new lambs in sun frost
survive another night,
skip towards summer

サンドラ・リニュー

モナロの原クーマへ
指せば子羊は
日に光る
霜に一夜を凌ぎて
夏へ跳びゆく

Luke Rigano

in tranquil grasslands
separated by vast seas
candles warm the soul

リューク・リガノ

静寂の草原
大洋に隔てられ
蝋燭魂を温む

Margaret Owen Ruckert　　　　マーガレット・オーエン・ルカート

sheep congregate
round the base of a tree trunk
white as bleached light,
as if paying respect
to the memory of shade

思い出の蔭を
尊ぶごとく
白く光る
幹の根元に
羊の集う

Ken Sheerin　　　　ケン・シアリン

the legend lives on...
historical films explained
on viewing Nara Park
– offspring of sacred white deer
now the gods' messengers

奈良公園の
聖なる鹿の
物語
歴史映画は
神の使者と説く

Catherine Smith　　　　キャサリン・スミス

New Year's Eve
in a long queue
a long wait
for the long ring
of this treasured bell

大晦日に
長き列なし
長く待つ
秘蔵の鐘の
長く響かむ

Carmel Summers　　　　　　　　カーメル・サマーズ

(at the Canberra Arboretum)　　「キャンベラ森林公園にて」

Japanese Snowbells　　　　　　藪スノーベル
one tree of many from　　　　　百国よりの
one hundred countries –　　　　一樹なり
sharing soil, water, climate　　　地、水、気候を分けあい
would that your bells ring for peace 平和の鐘つく

Rupert Summerson　　　　　　　ルパート・サマーソン

from Mount Ainslie's peak　　　　エンズリ山より見る
plum blossom threads the streets　梅の花の緑の街路を
in a green brocade　　　　　　　すくい取り
they weave into our city　　　　　春タピストリーの
a tapestry of spring　　　　　　　一枚に織る

Barbara Taylor　　　　　　　　　バーバラ・テイラー

lakeside strolls　　　　　　　　　湖畔ゆく
the joy of carillon bells　　　　　　歓鐘の鳴る
under azure skies　　　　　　　　蒼空に

Michael Thorley　　　　　　　マイクル・ソーリー

young city　　　　　　　　　花は咲く
ancient city　　　　　　　　　若き都に
cherry blossoms　　　　　　　旧都にも

Julie Thorndyke　　　　　　　ジュリー・ソーンダイク

an echidna　　　　　　　　　雪の中
trundles on thin snow　　　　　強い日ざしに
in strong sunlight –　　　　　　ハリネズミのそのそ歩む
a mixture of textures　　　　　この肌触り
only god could devise　　　　　まさしく神業

Paul Williamson　　　　　　　ポール・ウィリアムソン

high on the hill　　　　　　　　曇り空の
against the clouded sky　　　　丘にユーカリ
eucalypts huddle –　　　　　　ひしめきて
the talking tower points　　　　通信塔は
towards the hearing heavens　　天に語らう

Beatrice Yell　　　　　　　　ベアトリス・イェル

evening breeze　　　　　　　夕風の
skims over the lily pond...　　 睡蓮の池を
hotel guest　　　　　　　　　渡りゆく
and resident ibis　　　　　　　ホテルの客と常連アイビス
meet for a drink　　　　　　　飲みに集う
　　　　　　　　　　　　　　（註：アイビスは沼地に住む鳥）

slow movement　　　　　　　クラリネット
of a clarinet concerto –　　　　協奏曲のアダージオ
black swans on the lake　　　　湖上の黒鳥

Melodrama In Meiji Japan
明治時代のメロドラマ

The following sequence was inspired by the Kuchi-e exhibition held at the National Library of Australia (Canberra) from May to August 2017. Kuchi-e are the woodblock frontispiece illustrations from Meiji period novels.

以下の一連はキャンベラの国立図書館に於いて、2017年5月より8月まで、開催された「口絵展覧会」に触発されて書かれたものです。明治時代の小説本の口絵として木版画として刷られたイラストです。

chasing winter	展示室の
from the gallery	金屛風より
gilded screens	冬を追う

Heian princess	平安の
the face in the Kuchi-e	口絵の姫は
looks away	目をそらす

finding accord	孫の琴の
her grandchild plays Sakura	音探りつつ
on the koto	「桜」弾く

a woman's secret	桜板
pressed on the page	頁に刷らる
cherrywood block	女の秘密

cold wind	寒風や
through the blossom	花を透して
uplifting	高揚す

it might be Lake Burley Griffin ...but for kimono	バーリン・グリフィン湖 とも思えども 着物では...

The sequence was written by members of the Canberra region haiku group, known as Haiku@The Oaks. In order the authors were Marietta McGregor; Gregory Piko; Hazel Hall; Glenys Ferguson; Kathy Kituai; Jan Dobb.

句はHaiku@The Oaksと称するキャンベラ地区の俳句グループの会員によって作られました。作者は上から順を追って、マリエッタ・マックグレガー、グレゴリー・パイク、ヘイズル・ホール、グレニス・ファーガソン、キャシー・キクチュイ、ジャン・ドブ。

奈良篇

Nara Compilation

edited by Saeko Ogi and Noriko Tanaka
with English translations by Amelia Fielden

奈良と神仏　　　Nara and Divinities

櫟原聰　　　　　　Ichihala Satoshi

大仏は何度も炎の中にありてひとびとの願を受け止め来たる

> the Great Buddha,
> engulfed time after time
> by flames,
> remains acceptant
> of mankind's prayers

レリトー真美架 フランス　Mamika L'Heriteau (France)

奈良のたび夢違観音買ひしあと息子の悪夢たちまちきえぬ

> on a trip to Nara
> I bought a statue
> of Yumetagai Kannon,
> 'the Dream-breaker,' whereupon
> my son's nightmares ceased

歌崎功恵　　　　　Utazaki Norie

自らを善と信じる人の悪扱いがたく阿修羅像観る

> finding it hard
> to handle the evil
> of people
> who believe they are good,
> I gaze at a statue of Ashura

日比野美鈴　　　　　　Hibino Misuzu

たおやかな母なる如し伎芸天あいに来ました立ちあがるため

>to lift my spirits
>I am here to see
>Gigeiten,
>the Celestial Nymph who
>has the grace of a mother

橋本文子　　　　　　　Hashimoto Ayako

奈良の空そこぬけに青きこんな日は大仏様と散歩がしたい

>on such a day,
>when the sky over Nara
>is pure blue,
>I'd like to take a stroll
>with the Great Buddha

荒井公子　　　　　　　Arai Kimiko

うたげ終へ松明の火を振りこぼし帰られませり春日の神は

>celebration over,
>the Kasuga gods
>are returned
>to their shrine, sparks spilling
>from the pine torches

笹川幸震　　　　　　　Sasagawa Kōshin

本殿の軒に並びし吊り灯籠その数ほどの哀楽あらむ

> probably there are
> as many griefs and pleasures
> as there are lanterns
> hung in rows beneath the eaves
> of the Great Hall

橋本至紀子　　　　　　Hashimoto Shikiko

「春日大社節分万灯籠」

(Ten Thousand Lanterns at the end of winter at Kasuga Shrine)

回廊の釣灯籠の灯のともりいにしへの闇よみがへりくる

> the light from flames
> in the hanging lanterns
> along the cloisters
> is returning now
> to the darkness of old

肥田美咲(奈良大学大学生) Hida Misaki (university student)

古都奈良で修復学ぶこの手から小さな歴史を蘇らせたい

> in Nara, the old capital,
> I study restoration –
> with these hands of mine
> I want to be able to revive
> some small part of history

奈良の森　　The Forests of Nara

小黒　世茂　　　　　　Oguro Yomo

「こころ飛火野」　　　(Nostalgic Tobuhino)

山霧を風はらふときゆるやかに青ざめてゆく春日の森なり

> as breezes
> brush it with mist
> from the mountains,
> Kasuga forest
> is slowly paling

上田　倫子　　　　　　Ueda Michiko

飛火野をまろびつつ来る幼子は春の草生の光を踏めり

> trundling around
> the field of Tobuhino
> a child trod
> on the radiance
> of spring grasses

山田修子　　　　　　　Yamada Shūko

奈良に来れば春日の杜は色づきて精霊溢れ深く息する

> when I come to Nara
> and the Kasuga grove
> is changing colour,
> I feel spirits everywhere
> breathing deeply

奈良の山　　Nara Mountains

萩岡良博　　　　　　Hagioka Yoshihiro

つくよみにしろき稜線なめされて夜の食す国艶めきにけり

> white ridges
> are flattened
> by moonlight –
> we eat at night
> in the lustrous countryside

遠山 利子　　　　　Tōyama Toshiko

あかあかと炎(ひ)につつまるる若草山のくらき陰より春は生(あ)れ来む

> from the dark shadows
> of Wakakusa Mountain,
> wrapped all around
> in red, red flames
> spring will be born

高木佳子(潮音)　　　Takagi Yoshiko (Chōon Tanka Group)

この丘に見てゐる日の陽のあかあかとわがうちらにも灯しゆかむか

> perhaps the redness
> of this sun I'm seeing
> on the hill
> will light me
> internally also

兼築　信行　　　　　　Kanechiku Nobuyuki

うれしさにうま酒三輪の山を望み吾子の名前は弥和と定めき

> filled with happiness
> I drank sweet saké
> while gazing at Miwa Mountain,
> and decided my child's name
> would be Miwa

神子　直輝　奈良大学付属高校生
　　　　　　Kamiko Naoki (student)

奈良の山春夏秋冬変化して人の心に明るさともす

> the mountains of Nara
> transformed through spring,
> summer, autumn, winter,
> light lamps of brightness
> in our human hearts

奈良と動物

Nara and Animals

鹿

Deer

喜夛隆子

Kita Takako

妻を呼ぶ牡鹿のこゑの澄みわたり春日の森の夕闇ぞ濃し

> clear and pure
> the voice of a stag
> calling his mate
> bells through Kasuga forest
> as night's darkness deepens

久我久美子

Kuga Kumiko

神鹿の歩みゆるらに芝を踏む浅茅ヶ原は朝靄の中

> in the morning dew
> at Asajigahara field
> sacred deer
> amble slowly
> stepping on the grass

中村佳文

Nakamura Yoshifumi

せんべいを買ふ母の腰にうごめきて神にあらずや歯ぐきむく君

> naughty thing,
> squirming and snarling
> against my mother
> who buys you rice crackers,
> aren't you a god?

吉野節子　　　　　　　Yoshino Setsuko

堆き落葉のやまに身をうづめまなこ細める一頭の鹿

      a single deer
      with narrowed eyes
      burying herself
      in a mountain
      of fallen leaves

安田和子　　　　　　　Yasuda Kazuko

首すじのやさしき鹿も猛き角もちたる鹿も春日野の景

      in the scenery
      of Kasuga plain
      one views
      both deer with gentle necks
      and stags with fierce horns

稲川信恵　　　　　　　Inagawa Nobue

紅葉のしぐるる森に落葉食む鹿の胃の腑もあかあかと秋

      in the showery forest
      of scarlet leaves,
      the stomach of a deer
      that eats the fallen leaves
      must be as red as autumn

吉川仁子　　　　　　Yoshikawa Hitoko

雨の日の飛火野は全て鹿のもの音無く時無く絵画となりぬ

>on a rainy day
>the whole of Tobuhino
>belongs to the deer –
>it has become a painting
>soundless and timeless

浦晶　大阪芸大生　　Ura Aki (student)

金色に輝く丘で神さまの使いは軒並み寝てばかりいる

>on the hill
>glittering with golden light
>'messengers of the gods'
>one and all
>are doing nothing but sleep

能勢絢子　宮崎大生　Nose Ayako (student)

奈良のこと何にも知らないけど分かる　鹿のいるところ人のいるところ

>knowing
>nothing of Nara
>I just understand this:
>it's a place where
>both deer and people live

小田原滉紀　宮崎大生　　Odawara Kōki (student)

ヒトとかいう動物にひとつお辞儀して鹿界隈のエリートになる

                    bowing
                    to an animal
                    called 'human'
                    I am the elite
                    of this deer district

中山　郁弥　奈良大学附属高校生
                    Nakayama Fumiya (student)

春日野の若草茂る山肌に角をたてつつ鹿も鳴くかな

                    the mountain
                    behind Kasuga plain
                    is thick with young grass,
                    and there one hears the cries
                    of stags with erect horns

鳥　　　　　　　　　　Birds

米田靖子　　　　　　　Komeda Yasuko

雨のこる野分の空を乱舞なすわたりそこねし寧楽のツバメら

                    Nara swallows,
                    having missed their migration,
                    dance wildly
                    through the stormy sky
                    where rain still lingers

岡田淳　　　　　　　　　Okada Junichi

柿咥えカラスはどこに帰りゆく独りの旅の日は傾きぬ

       I wonder where
       they are returning, crows
       carrying persimmons
       in their beaks –
       the sun sets on my solo trip

蝉　　　　　　　　　　　Cicadas

島本太香子　奈良大教員奈良大短歌会
       Shimamoto Takako
       (Nara University Tanka Group)

春蝉を聴きて週末風邪に伏すまなうらに短音階の翠

       listening to spring cicadas
       on the weekend
       I lie in a bed with a cold –
       behind my eyes
       is the green of a minor scale

奈良の古き町並　Old Row Houses in Nara

松本実穂　フランス　　　　Matsumoto Miho (France)

伝へたきこともあらねどゆくりなく三条通りに便箋を買ふ

> though there is nothing
> that I want to say,
> unthinkingly
> I buy some writing paper
> on Sanjō street

石田郁男　フランス　　　　Ishida Ikuo (France)

はりつめた青空ふかく柿実る奈良にもどりし友のインスタ

> persimmons ripen
> deep in the expanse
> of the blue sky –
> an instagram from a friend
> who has come back to Nara

筒井幸子　　　　　　　　　Tsutsui Sachiko

嘴のある人奈良の路地に消ゆ赤銅色の月の夜なり

> a beaked person
> disappears from the Nara street –
> it's a night
> when the moon
> is a coppery red colour

鶴見セツ　　　　　　　Tsurumi Setsu

「売家」の立て看板の傾きを直しておりぬ友住みし家

> I was straightening
> the tilted billboard,
> 'house for sale',
> in front of the home
> where my friend had lived

舟橋伶子　　　　　　　Funahashi Reiko

雲一つなき如月の国道に大空団地（おほぞら）ゆきのバス待ちて佇つ

> under a cloudless sky
> in the second month
> I stand on the highway
> waiting for the bus
> that goes to the Ōzora Apartments

溝尾　智重子　　　　　Mizoo Chieko

木犀の香をふいに聞く無人駅しじま冷たき地下通路の秋

> suddenly I smell
> the scent of sweet osmanthus
> in the silence
> of an empty station
> underground, in autumn

田村京子　　　　　　　Tamura Kyōko

年深み墨色なせる塔の下風起こるなり奈良の風なり

          as the year passes,
          below the ink black pagoda
          the wind
          is rising...it is
          a Nara wind

仙田佳恵　　　　　　　Senda Yoshie

暮れの空は完璧すぎて　片を外してみたいジグソーパズル

          the darkening sky
          is too perfect –
          I want to remove
          one piece
          of the jigsaw puzzle

田村ふみ乃　　　　　　Tamura Fumino

まだ知らぬとら猫よぎりネコ地図にちさく点打つ榛原の路地

          a stray cat
          I hadn't yet met, crosses
          putting
          small dots on the cat map
          of Haibara alley

高山征三　メルボルン　　　Takayama Seizō (Melbourne)

韻韻と鐘の響ける古都の夕千年（ちとせ）の歴史ひもとく如く

                bong, bong
                the temple bell reverberates
                as if opening up
                a thousand years
                of the old capital's history

中島裕康　メルボルン　　　Nakajima Hiroyasu (Melbourne)

奈良町に迷い入りたる秋日和庚申さんに道を問はばや

                this autumn day
                I wander in confusion
                around Naramachi –
                I might ask the way
                of Kōshinsan, the Zodiac monkey

三宅眞理　　　　　　　　Miyake Mari

夕暮れに風に流さる白雲に戯れ別れつかめぬ夢路

                on my dream path
                I played with white clouds
                streaming in the wind
                through the dusk –
                unable to part

智内展子　　　　　　　　Chinai Nobuko

いにしえの奈良の都に来て思う地球の裏の真夏のサンタ

> come to Nara
> this ancient capital,
> I think
> of Santa Claus
> in midsummer, 'down-under'

御手洗靖大　同志社大生　Mitarai Yasuhiro (student)

約束の行基像前2時間も前から居ると言えるわけなく

> I've been here
> at the appointed place
> in front of Gyōki's statue
> for the last two hours –
> but I can't say that

倉永志　宮崎大生　　　　Kuranaga Kokoro (student)

「『金貯まるなり』じゃないじゃん」法隆寺子規の御前(みまえ)で十年を恥づ

> 'you can make money'
> you said, but I haven't –
> penitent, after ten years
> thinking at Horyūji
> of Shiki's haiku

Note: the poet is playing with the Japanese pun bell/money.

奈良の草花　　Nara's Wild Flowers

喜多弘樹　　　　　Kita Hiroki

考へる人のごとくに馬酔木(あしび)咲くぬばたまの夜の頬を撫づるも

                like a thinking person
                the ashibi flower blooms –
                a night
                as black as leopard seeds
                strokes my cheek

佐方三千枝　　　　Sakata Michie

とめどなく降りくる雪のまさらなるどのひとひらもむつの花びら

                ceaselessly falling
                the snow
                is pure white –
                every single flake
                has six petals

中里　葵　奈良大生　Nakazato Aoi

秋深く澄みたる空に映える金稲穂の波は風にさざめく

                shining
                against the clear sky
                of late autumn,
                golden-headed rice plants
                wave and ripple in the wind

奈良の月キャンベラの月 Moon in Nara, Moon in Canberra

後藤秀彦　　　　　　Gotō Hidehiko

月を見て何を思ふ奈良の月キャンベラの月戦場の月

> what do you think of
> when you look at the moon –
> the Nara moon,
> the Canberra moon,
> a battlefield moon

阿部　由花里　　　　Abe Yukari

冴え冴えと月照り渡る古都奈良は時の移ろい全て抱きとむ

> brilliantly the moon shines
> across Nara, the old capital
> that embraces
> and holds within itself
> all the times of the past

キャンベラの町と自然 Canberra City and Nature

アームストロングゆかり キャンベラ
      Armstrong Yukali (Canberra)

霧放つレイクジョージに沿い走る車窓の外はミルクの海よ

    beyond the windows
    of my car
    driving alongside,
    misty Lake George
    is a sea of milk

伊藤さと メルボルン Itoh Sato (Melbourne)

キャンベラの藤の花房言寄せて撮りて送らむ奈良の旧き友に

    prompted
    by Canberra's wisteria clusters
    I take a photo
    which I'll send with a letter
    to my old friend in Nara

ラム直子 キャンベラ Lamb Naoko (Canberra)

キャンベラの戦争記念館(ウォーメモリアル)に日本兵の持ちし日の丸収められをり

    in Canberra's War Memorial
    is preserved
    a Hinomaru flag
    that once belonged
    to a Japanese soldier

Note: the Japanese flag symbolises the rising sun.

加藤　皓　奈良大学附属高校生
Kato Kō (student)

奈良の空吹き上げられし木の葉舞うキャンベラの原青葉盛りに

                     leaves from Nara trees
                     blown high into the sky,
                     while the fields
                     of Canberra are full
                     of lush young leaves

www.ingramcontent.com/pod-product-compliance
Lightning Source LLC
Chambersburg PA
CBHW062206100526
44589CB00014B/1969